Wishing You...

... fa la la la la ...

Copyright© 1999 by Landauer Corporation

Art Copyright© 1999 by Sandi Gore Evans
This book was designed, produced, and published by Landauer Books
A division of Landauer Corporation
12251 Maffitt Road, Cumming, Iowa 50061

President: Jeramy Lanigan Landauer
Vice President: Becky Johnston
Managing Editor: Marlene Hemberger Heuertz
Art Director: Laurel Albright
Associate Editor: Sarah Reid
Graphics Technician: Stewart Cott

ISBN: 1-890621-07-2

Library of Congress Cataloging-in-Publication Data available on request.

This book is printed on acid-free paper.

Printed in Hong Kong

10 9 8 7 6 5 4 3 2 1

Wishing You...

Illustrated and Written by
Sandi Gore Evans

Welcome to a winter wonderland of holiday cheer
fresh from the pen and paintbrush
of Sandi Gore Evans!

It all starts in her backyard with the first snowfall...

Like most backyards, it is a place where
miracles happen and memories are made.
Inspired by loving family,
close friends and her cozy mid-western home,
Sandi shares with you the ABCs of
holiday wit and whimsy.

She hopes you will take a moment to enjoy this book
and reflect on the simple joys of the season with...

Blessings from
Sandi Gore Evans

Wishing You...

The Simple Joys of the Season

A ...the Aroma of a warm cup

of cocoa and cookies with sugar sprinkles.

B

...Bright shiny stars to place on top of the tree...
Beckoning to all...come, follow me.

Follow the Star.....

Cookies, Candy, and snow Cones
shared with a friend for a
very sweet day.

SNO
CONES
FRESH 10¢

D

...Inner peace each and every Day...one Day at a time.

...Evergreens, all decked out with twinkling lights...

and the drive around town to check it all out.

12

...Singing the songs of the season with Family and Friends.

...fa la la la la

...fa la la la la ...

13

...the Glee Club...God Loves each and everyone...and wants us to love one another.

And..Heaven and Nature Sing...

...Hope, within each seed is the

memory of springtimes past,
and the promise of all things new.

...Incredible snowflakes...each one a miracle, different from the other.

© '94 Sandi Gore Evans

 ...Joy, Joy, Joy,
Joy down in my .

K...Knowing that good friends will always be there... even when my whole world is turning upside down.

The Luxury of warm, dry socks and mittens (matchng is best).

M

...Roasting Marshmallows for smores

SMORES
5¢

and debating whether
they should be toasty brown or black.

...the rosey cheeks and Noses of children and tissues!

GLEE

O ...Christmas Ornaments...made by little hands

Or passed down from One generation to the next.

P...All of life's surprises...no Peeking!

...Snuggling up in grandma's Quilt...

A blanket of snow and a warm cozy quilt

and peace...and Quiet.

R ...Redbirds, and chick-a-dees and sparrows that sit on my window feeder. (If only I could fly!)

S...Seed catalogues that arrive in the winter... daydreaming on a gray - sky - day.

...Traditions...knowing that we are a part of our forefathers and our grandchildren.

"...Standing Under... the mistletoe.

Merry Kissmas

...Little Voices that giggle with delight

when Santa has come and gone.

Evans

...Sending Warm Wishes Your Way

XYZ

zzzzz...

...For Yuletide blessings and the simple joys of the season.

Wishing You...Happy Endings